BIRTHDAYS
and family
CELEBRATIONS

Better Homes and Gardens

MEREDITH PRESS

BETTER HOMES AND GARDENS CREATIVE COOKING LIBRARY, FIRST PRINTING

Garden Row Cupcakes come straight from the land where lollipops grow on trees—to delight every birthday child who ever read Hansel and Gretel!

Contents

Cake of the Dancing Dolls. Easy
cutouts, candles in gumdrop
holders give celebration look

Spring Bonnet Cake. Chic with
stylish marshmallow daisies

Birthdays

Here are cake recipes you'll treasure . . . fast
candy trims to do you proud . . . marvelous
ice-cream concoctions . . . dozens of party ideas!

Parties for the kids!

Birthday parties are fun! They needn't be elaborate. Any time three children get together with paper hats, balloons, and cookies, it's a party! Just a little preparation will make it a party to remember.

Invitations

Make small folders of colored paper. Paste a small snapshot of the birthday child on the outside. Write in white ink on the inside, a rhyme about his birthday, age, and the time of party.

Another idea. On plain envelope print this jingle: "A birthday party there will be—Blow up the balloon and you will see." Inflate small balloons and write with a ball point pen the necessary information: "At Karen's house—Wednesday, the 5th, 3:30 to 5:00." Deflate balloons, seal in the envelopes and deliver to guests.

Decorations

The table with its cake centerpiece, brightly colored favors and napkins, and the birthday gifts in their gay wrappings are usually all the decoration needed for birthday parties. Flowers in season are nice, but their containers should be placed high (on mantel or chest) so they won't be tipped over. Colorful, gas-filled balloons hovering against the ceiling add a gala note to any party.

If possible, seat all the children at one large table. Use a paper tablecloth or plastic place mats. Colored paper plates and plastic spoons add to the gay appearance of the table and cut cleaning and dishwashing time for you.

For place-markers, write each guest's name on his glass with bright red nail polish. The names can be removed later with nail-polish remover. Or paint name on balloon; tie it with a string to his chair.

Entertainment

Allow 15 or 20 minutes for the arrival of stragglers and the opening of gifts. If children are very young, read a lively story or play an appropriate record.

After things quiet down, serve the refreshments. Then start games. The best games for little children are those with a familiar foundation, but a new twist. Here's a variation of musical chairs: Seat guests in a large circle on the floor. Give the first child an inexpensive sand pail and shovel. Start music and let the children pass the pail and shovel around the circle using both hands, until the music is stopped suddenly. The child holding the pail is dropped from the circle. The game continues until only one child remains. He wins the pail and shovel. If any child drops the shovel from the pail in passing it, he is eliminated from the game.

A final game might be "Treasure Hunt." Have small favors hidden around the room. Have the children search for them, with the rule that no one may have more than two favors (or whatever limit you choose). This way no child goes home empty-handed.

You'll find more ideas on the next few pages for parties the kids will never forget. These first parties are the stuff that marvelous childhood memories are made of!

Happy ending!

Give each child a decorated paper bag, or a plastic bag, in which he can carry home his "loot"—prizes, favors, candy, balloon. This also makes cleaning up much easier.

A cupcake party!

Small guests demonstrate their cake-decorating skill with unfrosted cupcakes.

Bowls of the frosting and trims form the centerpiece; children "paint" the cupcakes. (Provide paper aprons and caps.) The rules permit one cake to be eaten!

Giant-land dinner party

Children just love feeling bigger than they are, so let them! They're giant-size at this party. Use the tiniest dolls (for people), cup and saucers to suit them, and demitasse spoons. Arrange on a big square of cardboard in center of the floor—giant people will tower over the table!

Favors are dolls' hats. Menu consists of thimble-size hamburgers on little biscuits, thumb-size scoops of ice cream made with melon scoop, and inch-square bits of cake.

Bus-to-Bermuda party

"Party" buses are available through many city transit or school bus companies. And you'll find they don't cost a fortune. It's a fine way to give a party for a group when your own party-giving space is limited.

Bus jaunts offer a variety of fun. Any place from a museum to a cider mill is a delightful experience for children. Birthday child can be "pop" vendor on the bus ride with the group returning home for refreshments.

Pirate party

Ho-ho and a bottle of pop! Pirates haven't been around for quite some time, but a children's pirate party will never be out of date.

Feature a treasure hunt with clues written on skillfully aged paper (a little smudging and dirt will do the trick). Bags of pennies, marbles, and rubber daggers make good prizes.

Topsy-turvy party

This is good fun for all ages. To begin with, you greet guests with "goodbye, I'm so glad you had a good time" . . . and carry on from there.

Eat the dessert first and the sandwiches last . . . if it's winter, wear summer clothes, if it's summer, wear snowsuits and galoshes. Topsy-turvy games really take care of themselves. And who couldn't set a turnabout table! Trick-store glasses (the kind where the water won't come out) set upside down are a great help.

Cartoon character party

Kids know all the comic-strip characters, and can be depended on to come dressed as their favorite.

Games should have a cartoon theme—Donald Duck treasure hunt or Dagwood "string-eating" contest. Food: Wimpy-burgers.

Train to Nowhere

Perfect party for energetic little boys! Place a small train made from cardboard boxes decorated to resemble various cars of a train—engine, coal car, boxcar, and so forth—in the center of your room. (The boxcar makes an excellent container for presents.) Divide the group into railroad crews, engineer, brakeman, fireman; supply each with appropriate hats. Let each crew take a part of the train outdoors and fill it with proper freight from designated locations in your neighborhood.

Whistle your train crew home when it's time for refreshments. If you've an electric train, use it for a table centerpiece, moving up and down the table to dispense tidbits for hungry conductors.

Artists' Colony Party

Use the back yard with large sheets of white paper tacked to the fence. Collect as many worn-out men's shirts as you have guests—they make excellent smocks for pint-size Picassos.

Provide each painter with a long brush and a couple of glasses of premixed poster paint. You'll have a Greenwich Village art show in no time at all! A committee of parents can pin ribbons on the best paintings.

Set up a group of card tables covered with red-checked tablecloths and give them something hearty like spaghetti to eat.

Puzzle Party

It's a costume jamboree! Guests dress as a book character, someone from television or the movies, or even an advertising slogan. Part of the fun is guessing who's who.

Games are along the puzzle line. It's even more fun when they're homemade. Give each child simple scenes cut out and backed with cardboard. Have a time limit for putting it together. Put up faces of personalities, familiar slogans, camouflaged magazine covers to be identified. Set up a long table with puzzle jars filled with beans, noodles, peanuts, etc., and have the party people make guesses. Rent two identical big jigsaw puzzles, divide the group, see who puts them together first.

Circus Party

Balloons are a natural here. By rubbing the inflated balloons against your clothing for a minute, you will create enough static to make them adhere to the walls. If there's an artist in the family, ask for painted circus posters of bareback riders, trapeze performers, and so on. And anyone can draw on a big sheet of butcher paper a large-scale clown's face, with gaping mouth. Top the face with the pomponed, peaked clown's hat. Fasten the clown to the side of a large cardboard box; cut a hole in the box for the clown's open mouth. At game time, have the children toss table tennis balls or jelly beans into the clown's mouth.

Have guests be circus performers. Write stunts on slips of paper and let each child pick one. Then they take turns doing their stunt: walking a straight line for a tightrope; dancing like a clown or a trained dog; walking on all fours, swinging head to imitate an elephant; roaring like a lion.

Youngsters in Wonderland

"Alice" is never out-of-date—the "curious" things that happen to her are forever intriguing. So an afternoon in "Wonderland" is a delightful kind of party.

Send invitations in looking-glass writing (write place cards backwards, too.) For the party entrance, cover a cardboard barrel with grass cloth and place it in the doorway (fill the space above with crepe paper streamers); children crawl through "rabbit hole" to get into party room.

Remove all breakables and cover furniture with sheets. Decorate a la Alice—make cardboard cutouts to resemble the frock-coated bespeckled rabbit, the Queen, the Mad Hatter, and the like. Your Christmas tree lights will add an eerie glow.

For games—take a cue from the book (re-read it if you need to); try checkerboard hopscotch where the person who wins loses, and padded croquet mallets made of wire hangers and used like pick-up sticks!

Your table can look like the Mad Hatter's tea party, with white paper pinafores for the girls and Mad Hatter cardboard hats for the boys.

Glorious birthday cakes

Garden Row Cupcakes (page 4)

Line bottoms of 8 or 9 new clay flower pots (2½ inches high) with small circles of foil or waxed paper. Fill with vanilla ice cream—you'll need 3 pints ice cream. Wrap ends of 4½-inch peppermint-stick candy in clear plastic wrap; poke in center of each flower pot. Freeze firm.

Mix and bake 1 recipe Cupcakes; cool thoroughly. Prepare 1 recipe Butter-cream Frosting (page 17). With food coloring, tint *half* the frosting pink, the other *half* yellow. (See page 37).

Frost cupcakes on bottom and sides. Roll in matching color coconut. Now frost tops.

At serving time, place small piece clear plastic wrap over end of candy sticks; poke into cupcakes. Sprinkle ice cream with chocolate decorettes. Serve at once. Makes 8 or 9 servings.

Cupcakes: Stir ⅓ cup shortening to soften. Sift in 2 cups sifted cake flour, 1 cup sugar, 2½ teaspoons baking powder, and ¾ teaspoon salt. Measure ¾ cup milk; add *half* to mixture. Add 1 slightly beaten egg. Mix till flour is dampened.

Beat 2 minutes at low speed on electric mixer. Add remaining milk and 1 teaspoon vanilla; beat 1 minute longer.

Fill small greased muffin pans (2¼ inches in diameter) ½ full. Bake in moderate oven (375°) about 20 minutes or till done. Cool thoroughly; remove from pans.

Lollipop Birthday Cake (see cover)

For our cover cake, we grew a garden of lollipops—one for each child at the party. Lollipop sticks are slipped inside cellophane straws—no sticky fingers! For leaves, use gumdrop spearmint leaves. Under 7-minute Frosting, use Best Two-egg Cake.

Spring Bonnet Cake (page 7)

Fill and frost layers of Chiffon Layer Cake (page 14) with Pineapple 7-minute Frosting (page 17).

Marshmallow Daisies: Press big soft marshmallows lightly to flatten a bit; snip petals; center with small yellow gumdrops (toothpicks tack them in place).

Gumdrop Bows: Between sheets of waxed paper, roll out 2 large green gumdrops in long strips (have sugar on both sides of candy). Cut strips lengthwise in half; trim ½ inch wide. For each loop of bow, bend one end of strip back and tuck behind Marshmallow Daisy in center of hat brim (frosting will hold in place). Complete bow by adding two strips with pointed ends.

Best Two-egg Cake

Stir ½ cup butter, margarine, or shortening to soften. Gradually add 1½ cups sugar, and cream thoroughly 12 to 15 minutes at medium-high speed on electric mixer. Add 1 teaspoon vanilla, ¼ teaspoon lemon extract, and 2 or 3 drops almond extract. Add 2 eggs, one at a time; beat well after each.

Sift 2¼ cups sifted cake flour with 2½ teaspoons baking powder and 1 teaspoon salt. Add to creamed mixture alternately with 1 cup plus 2 tablespoons milk, beginning and ending with flour mixture, and beating after each addition.

Bake in 2 paper-lined 9x1½-inch round pans at 375° about 23 minutes or till done. Cool 5 minutes; remove from pans.

Note: For Drum Cake use 1½ times recipe; bake in three 9x1½-inch round pans.

with easy trims

Drum Cake—strike up the band for this one!
For the base of the drum, use our
Best Two-egg Cake. Cover with Butter-cream
Frosting. Use candy sugar sticks at
sides and as drumsticks, up top, with
sour-ball ends. Light a tall red candle.

Chiffon Layer Cake

2 egg whites
½ cup sugar

• • •

2¼ cups sifted cake flour
1 cup sugar
3 teaspoons baking powder
1 teaspoon salt
⅓ cup salad oil
1 cup milk
1½ teaspoons vanilla
2 egg yolks

Beat egg whites till foamy. Gradually beat in ½ cup sugar. Continue beating till very stiff and glossy. Sift remaining dry ingredients into another bowl; add salad oil, *half* of the milk, and the vanilla. Beat 1 minute at medium speed on mixer or 150 strokes by hand, scraping sides and bottom of bowl constantly.

Add remaining milk and egg yolks. Beat 1 minute longer, scraping bowl constantly. Gently fold in egg-white mixture with down-up-and-over motion, turning bowl.

Bake in 2 paper-lined 9x1½-inch round pans in moderate oven (350°) 25 to 30 minutes. Cool thoroughly; remove from pans.

White Cake

¾ cup shortening
1½ cups sugar

• • •

1½ teaspoons vanilla
2¼ cups sifted cake flour
3 teaspoons baking powder
1 teaspoon salt
1 cup milk
5 stiff-beaten egg whites

Stir shortening to soften. Gradually add sugar, and cream together till light and fluffy (beat about 10 minutes at medium-high speed on electric mixer, scraping the bowl occasionally to guide the batter into the beaters). Add the vanilla.

Sift flour with baking powder and salt; add to creamed mixture alternately with milk, beginning and ending with flour mixture, and beating after each addition. Beat 2 minutes at medium speed. Fold in egg whites. Bake in 2 paper-lined 9x1½-inch round pans in moderate oven (375°) 18 to 20 minutes. Cool 5 minutes; remove from pans. Cool thoroughly.

Cake of the Dancing Dolls
(*page 6*)

Fill and frost layers of White Cake with Strawberry Frosting. Center with a ring of Dancing Dolls, as pictured on page 6. Around cake, arrange red birthday candles in Gumdrop Petal Holders.

Dancing Dolls: We used a strip of bright pink paper, 19¼x4 inches. At narrow side, make a fold 2⅛ inches wide for a measure, then fold the paper over and over on itself till you come to end of strip. Now fold double to make narrow panel. On open side, snip out a half-silhouette, leaving attached at braids, hands, and skirt hems. Unfold—you'll have 9 dolls! Fasten first and last dolls with cellophane tape to make. circle. (For cutest dolls, cut 'em chubby, and don't forget to round the cheeks between braids and neck.)

Gumdrop Petal Holders: For each you'll need 2 fat gumdrops in different shades of the same color—we chose pink and red. (If the candy is soft, let stand overnight to dry a little.) From the outside of each gumdrop, snip off 5 long petals and overlap sticky-side up, bending upward to form flowers. Pinch end of each petal to shape. Press a pink flower inside a red, and insert birthday candle firmly in center.

Devil's Food Cake

⅔ cup shortening
2¼ cups sifted cake flour
2 cups sugar
1 teaspoon salt
1 teaspoon soda
1 teaspoon baking powder

• • •

1¼ cups milk
3 eggs
3 1-ounce squares unsweetened
   chocolate, melted

Stir shortening just to soften. Sift in dry ingredients. Add ½ *cup* of the milk; mix till all flour is dampened. Beat vigorously 2 minutes. Stir in remaining milk, the eggs, melted chocolate, and 1 teaspoon red food coloring. Beat vigorously 2 minutes longer. Bake in 2 paper-lined 8x8x2-inch square pans in moderate oven (350°) 35 to 40 minutes or till done. Cool 5 minutes and remove from pans.

Cake Canaveral with a chocolate launching pad!

Send your little spaceman into orbit

with this Devil's Food Cake with Chocolate Cream-cheese

Frosting. Use halved chocolate mints for radar

When it is time to blast off, light the candle rocket and let your spaceboy start the countdown— 10, 9, 8, 7, 6, 5, 4, 3, 2, 1. Pow! The cake will be demolished by happy munchers.

Chocolate Cream-cheese Frosting: Blend one 3-ounce package cream cheese, softened, and ¼ cup soft butter. Stir in 3¼ cups sifted confectioners' sugar, dash salt, ½ teaspoon vanilla, two 1-ounce squares unsweetened chocolate, melted, and 2 tablespoons milk. Beat smooth. Add just enough more milk to make of spreading consistency. Frosts tops and sides of two 8-inch square or round layers.

Parasol Cake brings showers of praise! Open some parasols, leave others partly shut. Hidden under parasols and Marshmallow Frosting is fresh, tender Orange Sponge Cake.

Orange Sponge Cake

6 egg yolks
1 tablespoon grated orange peel
½ cup orange juice
1½ cups sugar
¼ teaspoon salt
1⅛ cups sifted cake flour
6 egg whites
1 teaspoon cream of tartar

Beat yolks till thick and lemon-colored. Add peel and juice; beat till very thick. Gradually beat in *1 cup* sugar and the salt. Carefully fold in flour. Beat egg whites till foamy; add cream of tartar; beat to soft peaks. Gradually add remaining ½ *cup* sugar, beating to stiff peaks. Thoroughly fold whites into yolk mixture. Bake in *ungreased* 10-inch tube pan at 325° for 55 minutes or till done. Invert pan and cool.

7-minute Frosting

2 unbeaten egg whites
1½ cups sugar
2 teaspoons light corn syrup
   or ¼ teaspoon cream of tartar
⅓ cup cold water
Dash salt
1 to 1½ teaspoons vanilla

Place all ingredients except vanilla in top of double boiler (not over heat); beat 1 minute with electric or rotary beater to blend. Place over boiling water and cook, beating constantly, till frosting forms stiff peaks, *about* 7 minutes (*don't overcook*). Remove from boiling water. Pour into mixing bowl, if you wish. Add vanilla; beat till of spreading consistency, about 2 minutes. Frosts two 8- or 9-inch layers.

Peppermint 7-minute Frosting (for Lollipop Birthday Cake): In recipe above, decrease vanilla to ½ teaspoon; add ¼ teaspoon peppermint extract. Tint frosting pale pink with few drops red food coloring.

Pineapple 7-minute Frosting (for Spring Bonnet Cake): Substitute canned unsweetened pineapple juice for water in 7-minute Frosting. Tint frosting pale yellow with yellow food coloring.

Strawberry Frosting (for Cake of the Dancing Dolls). Add one-half 3-ounce package (3½ tablespoons) strawberry-flavored gelatin to sugar for 7-minute Frosting *before* cooking.

Marshmallow Frosting

Beat together one 1-pint jar marshmallow creme, 2 egg whites, 2 tablespoons water, and 1 teaspoon vanilla, at high speed on electric mixer till *very* stiff peaks form. Scrape sides of bowl often with rubber spatula. Frosts top and sides of one 10-inch tube cake or two 9-inch layers.

Butter-cream Frosting

In small bowl of electric mixer, blend one 1-pound package confectioners' sugar, sifted, ⅓ cup soft butter or margarine, ¼ cup milk, and 1 teaspoon vanilla.

Beat at medium speed 1 to 2 minutes, scraping bowl and beaters often with rubber spatula. (If stiff, add a little more milk to make of spreading consistency.) Frosts tops and sides of two 8- or 9-inch layers.

Hints for fabulous frosting

For smooth butter frosting cream butter: add confectioners' sugar *slowly*, beating smooth. To catch spills: Put 4 strips of waxed paper covering only plate edges. When cake is frosted, pull paper out.

Seven-minute tips: Boiling water should not touch top pan of double boiler. Beat frosting *about* 7 minutes. Remove from water when stiff peaks form.

Crumbs behave if you cover sides and top edge of cooled cake with thin layer of frosting. Spread on more—crumbs won't mix with second coat. Frost top of cake last.

For a teen-ager's birthday,

a soda-fountain special!

Snack Time for Teens

Submarine Sandwich Express
Relishes   Potato Chips
Hot Buttered Popcorn
Giant-size Sweet Rolls
Raspberry Flips   *or*   Pink Sodas
or your choice of sodas, sundaes, and shakes!

Submarine Sandwich Express

1 loaf French bread (about 20 inches long)
½ cup butter or margarine
1 clove garlic, minced
Tomato slices
Cheese slices, cut in half
Thin sliced Bologna or corned beef
Green-pepper rings (optional)

Cut bread in ¾-inch slices, *not quite through* bottom crust. Cream butter with minced garlic. Sprinkle tomato slices with salt. Spread garlic butter on facing sides of every other slice and insert tomato slice, half slice cheese, Bologna slice, and green-pepper ring, all in the same "pocket." Heat on cooky sheet in moderate oven (350°) 20 minutes. To serve, break or cut through bottom crust of unfilled slices. Makes 10 servings.

Raspberry Flips

2 10-ounce packages frozen red raspberries,
    thawed and sieved
1 quart vanilla ice cream
3 cups *cold* milk

Add raspberries to *half* the ice cream; beat smooth. Add milk and blend. Pour into 6 chilled 10-ounce glasses. Top each with scoop of remaining ice cream.

The young set puts on a wingding!

A mile-long sandwich loaf leads off the snack list, along with plenty of nibbles. "Soda jerk" whips up wonderful concoctions, serves them in honest-to-goodness soda glasses.

Fountain fix-ups

Minted Sundae Soda

Mint and lime flavors give double refreshment! Serve this beautiful half-sundae half-soda with both straw and spoon—

> 1 10-ounce jar (about 1 cup) mint apple jelly
> ½ cup water
>
> • • •
>
> Lime sherbet
> Vanilla ice cream
> Bottled lemon-lime carbonated beverage, chilled

Combine jelly and water in saucepan. Cook and stir over low heat till jelly dissolves. Cool, then chill. Into each chilled 14-ounce glass, pour about 3 tablespoons mint-jelly syrup. Add spoonful of sherbet or ice cream; stir till melted. Add scoop of vanilla ice cream, then scoop of lime sherbet, finally another scoop of vanilla ice cream. Fill with lemon-lime carbonated beverage, pouring carefully down side of glass to save sparkle. Garnish each glass with lime slices and a mint sprig.

Note: You may make this soda using 2 teaspoons bottled creme-de-menthe syrup in each glass, in place of mint-jelly syrup.

Minted Sundae Soda

Save the bubbles—they add refreshing sparkle and zing! At the last minute, just before serving, carefully pour the carbonated beverage down the *side* of the glass.

For soda success begin by muddling a little amount of the sherbet or ice cream with the sundae sauce. *And* you'll want to serve sodas with both straws and long-handled spoons.

Mint Malt

3 tablespoons crushed peppermint-stick candy
1½ cups milk
¼ cup chocolate-flavored malted-milk powder
Dash salt
1 teaspoon vanilla

• • •

1 pint chocolate ice cream

Place *half* of the crushed candy, ½ *cup of* the milk, the malted milk, salt, and vanilla in mixer bowl or blender. Blend until candy dissolves. Add ice cream; blend till softened. Add *1 cup* milk; mix just till blended. Pour into 4 chilled glasses. Top with whipped cream. Sprinkle with remaining crushed candy. Serve with candy sticks for muddlers.

Patio Punch Soda

1 46-ounce can (6 cups) red Hawaiian fruit punch, chilled
¾ cup lemon juice
1 quart vanilla ice cream
2 7-ounce bottles (2 cups) lemon-lime carbonated beverage, chilled

Combine punch and lemon juice. Spoon about *half* the ice cream into 9 or 10 chilled tall glasses. Add *half* the punch; muddle with ice cream. Add remaining punch; tip each glass and pour carbonated beverage down *side* to fill. Top each with a scoop of ice cream. Trim with lemon peel.

Pink Sodas

For each "customer," place jumbo scoop of vanilla or strawberry ice cream in tall glass. Fill with chilled strawberry carbonated beverage. Serve with long straws.

Chocolate Soda

For each serving, pour ¼ cup chocolate syrup and 2 tablespoons milk into a chilled 14- or 16-ounce glass; mix well. Add chilled carbonated water to fill glass ¾ full. Stir. Add 1 to 2 scoops vanilla ice cream. Fill with carbonated water. Serve.

Chocolate Shake

Combine ½ cup *cold* milk and 2 tablespoons chocolate syrup in chilled mixing bowl or blender. Add 2 big scoops vanilla ice cream, beating or blending until smooth. Makes 1 serving.
Note: For a malted milk, add 1 tablespoon malted-milk powder after the milk.

Grape Frost

1 6-ounce can frozen grape-lemon punch concentrate
About 5 to 6 cups finely crushed ice

Empty frozen concentrate into chilled bowl of an electric blender. Add ice, 1 cup at a time, blending well after each addition. Stop blender several times and push ice down with rubber scraper. Serve at once.

Citrus Cooler

Ginger ale is the sparkle in this refreshing fruit fizz. You'll make this often—

¼ cup frozen orange-grapefruit-juice concentrate
¾ cup ice water
1 pint lemon sherbet
1 12-ounce bottle (1½ cups) ginger ale, chilled

Pour frozen orange-grapefruit-juice concentrate into an electric blender or drink mixer. Add ice water and sherbet. Cover and blend about 15 seconds.

Divide mixture among 3 or 4 chilled glasses. Slowly pour in ginger ale to fill each glass. Stir gently and serve right away.

Raspberry Parfaits

Prechill parfait glasses till frosty cold. For the sundae sauce, use frozen red raspberries, thawed, but with *a few ice crystals remaining.* (Or use sweetened crushed fresh raspberries.) Save out some whole berries for garnish.

Start parfaits with a big spoonful of the raspberries and syrup in bottom of each glass. Add scoop of raspberry ice cream or strawberry or vanilla. Alternate layers of raspberries and ice cream. Top with whipped cream and whole berries.

Big Banana Split

Fully ripe bananas
Canned pineapple slices, chilled
Three flavors of ice cream or sherbet— strawberry, vanilla, and orange
Three sundae sauces—Raspberry Sundae Sauce, chocolate sauce, and marshmallow creme
Bing cherries or maraschino cherries with stems on

Count on 1 banana, halved lengthwise and peeled, for each split. Drain pineapple, and dip bananas in the pineapple syrup to keep color bright. Place a pineapple ring in the center of each *long* dish. Now add a banana runner on each side.

Top pineapple ring with a scoop of orange sherbet, add a scoop of vanilla ice cream on one side, a scoop of strawberry on the other. Cut a pineapple ring in half and tuck in, like wings, between the scoops.

Ladle Raspberry Sundae Sauce over vanilla ice cream, chocolate sauce over strawberry, marshmallow creme over orange sherbet. Then for good measure, flood dish with all three sauces. Trim with cherries.

Raspberry Sundae Sauce

Stir a jar of red-raspberry preserves to make it of just-right spooning consistency to ladle over ice cream. That's all!

Pretty ice-cream slices or sundaes—here's how it's done

A cake breaker makes neat slices, even in the firmest ice cream. Neapolitan ice cream shows off three ribbons of color. Another time, cut ice cream in wedges. To help keep servings from melting, chill plates.

Here's how spectacular sundaes get that rippled look. Chill sturdy spoon in freezer. Holding it bowl up, skim across firm ice cream. Start fudge sundae with scoop of ice cream in *chilled* dish; alternate light and dark.

Banana Nog

1 medium fully ripe banana
½ pint (1 cup) vanilla ice cream
1 6-ounce can (⅔ cup) evaporated
   milk, chilled
1 egg
1 teaspoon vanilla

Combine ingredients in electric blender or drink mixer. Whiz about 30 seconds or till blended. Pour into 2 chilled glasses. Sprinkle with nutmeg. Serve with straws.

Butterscotch Sauce

Combine 1½ cups brown sugar, ⅔ cup corn syrup, and dash salt. Heat, stirring occasionally, till mixture comes to a full rolling boil. Remove from heat; cool slightly. Gradually stir in one 6-ounce can (⅔ cup) evaporated milk. Serve warm or cool. Makes 2 cups sauce.

Crunchy Butterscotch Sundaes

Mix 1½ cups sugar-coated crisp rice or wheat cereal with ½ cup flaked coconut. Form 1 quart vanilla ice cream in 10 balls. Coat with cereal mixture, pressing it on. Place in freezer till serving time. (To keep coating crisp, store only 1 to 4 hours.) Serve with Butterscotch Sauce. Makes 10 servings.

Fudge Sundae

Start out with enough fudge sauce in each dish to cover bottom generously. In center place hub of chocolate or vanilla ice cream. Then overlap 4 big spoonfuls of ice cream around it, alternating light and dark.

Drizzle more sundae sauce over top. Sprinkle with broken California walnuts.

Honey-Fudge Sauce

Melt 2 squares unsweetened chocolate with ½ cup honey over hot water. Add dash salt; stir till smooth. Spoon hot sauce over ice cream.

Choco-Mint Sauce

Melt 12 chocolate-covered mint patties (about 1½ inches in diameter) over hot water. Stir in 2 tablespoons light cream. Serve warm over ice cream. Makes ½ cup sauce.

Mintmallow Sauce

Combine about ½ cup marshmallow creme and 3 tablespoons water. With electric or rotary beater, whip till fluffy.

Add ¼ cup mint jelly and beat smooth. Tint with few drops green food coloring. Spoon over vanilla or chocolate ice cream. Makes about 2 cups sauce.

You'll welcome this pair of slick tricks for ice-cream dips

Double-color dips boast double flavors! Work with firm ice cream, and a chilled scoop. Half-fill scoop by taking several light scoops in one flavor, then round out ball with another flavor. Serve with sundae sauce.

Serving ice cream to a crowd? Fix the scoops beforehand; place on jelly-roll pan or cooky sheet; put uncovered in freezer. To serve, place ice-cream balls in bowl. (To keep a day or so, wrap and store in freezer.)

Grown-up birthday party

Big Birthday Dinner

Roast Rock Cornish Game Hens
Wild Rice   Creamed Mushrooms
Buttered Broccoli Spears
Greengage Plum Salad
Butterhorn Rolls   Butter
Burnt-sugar Cake *or* Angel Cake
Ice Cream   Coffee

Roast Rock Cornish Game Hens

Season four 1-pound ready-to-cook Rock Cornish game hens inside and out with salt and pepper. Stuff each with ¼ cup stuffing, if desired. Place, breast up, on rack in shallow roasting pan and brush well with ⅓ cup melted butter. Roast uncovered in hot oven (400°) about 1 hour or till done.

During last 15 minutes of baking time, baste several times with mixture of ¼ cup canned condensed consomme and ¼ cup light corn syrup. Makes 4 servings.

Greengage Plum Salad

1 No. 2½ can greengage plums
1 3-ounce package lemon-flavored gelatin
1 3-ounce package lime-flavored gelatin
1 cup finely chopped celery
1 3-ounce package cream cheese, softened
3 tablespoons light cream
1 tablespoon mayonnaise

Drain plums, reserving syrup; sieve plums. Add water to syrup to make 3½ cups; heat. Add gelatin, stir to dissolve. Add plums.

Chill till partially set; stir in celery. Turn into 8x8x2-inch pan. Blend remaining ingredients. Spoon atop; swirl through to marble. Chill firm. Cut in 9 or 12 squares.

Angel Cake

1 cup sifted cake flour
¾ cup sugar

• • •

1½ cups (12) egg whites
1½ teaspoons cream of tartar
¼ teaspoon salt
1½ teaspoons vanilla
¾ cup sugar

Sift flour with ¾ cup sugar 4 times. Beat egg whites with cream of tartar, salt, and vanilla till stiff enough to form soft peaks but still moist and glossy. Add the remaining ¾ cup sugar, 2 tablespoons at a time, beating until meringue holds stiff peaks.

Sift about ¼ of flour mixture over whites; fold in. Fold in remaining flour by fourths. Bake in *ungreased* 10-inch tube pan in moderate oven (375°) 35 to 40 minutes or till done. Invert pan; let cake cool thoroughly. Frost with your choice of our 7-minute frostings—see them on page 17.

Burnt-sugar Cake

½ cup shortening
2½ cups sifted cake flour
1½ cups sugar
3½ teaspoons baking powder
½ teaspoon salt
1 cup water
3 tablespoons Burnt-sugar Syrup
2 eggs
1 teaspoon vanilla

Stir shortening just to soften. Sift in dry ingredients. Add ⅔ *cup of the water;* mix until all flour is dampened. Then beat vigorously 2 minutes. Add remaining water, 3 tablespoons Burnt-sugar Syrup, eggs and vanilla; beat 2 minutes longer. Bake in 2 paper-lined 9x1½-inch round pans in moderate oven (375°) about 20 minutes or until done.* Cool 10 minutes; remove from pans. When thoroughly cool, fill with Date Filling and frost with Burnt-sugar Frosting. Press broken California walnuts on sides.

*Or bake in 2 paper-lined 8x1½-inch round pans at 350° about 30 minutes.

Burnt-sugar Frosting

　2 egg whites
　1¼ cups sugar
　3 to 4 tablespoons Burnt-sugar
　　Syrup*
　¼ cup cold water
　Dash salt
　1 teaspoon vanilla

Place all ingredients except vanilla in top of double boiler (not over heat); beat 1 minute with electric or rotary beater. Place over boiling water and cook, beating constantly, until mixture forms peaks, *about* 7 minutes (*don't overcook*). Remove from boiling water. Add vanilla and beat till of spreading consistency, about 2 minutes. Reserve ¼ cup frosting for Date Filling. Use remaining frosting on cake.

　*If you have a sweet tooth, use only 3 tablespoons; if you like a "touch of bitter," try 4 tablespoons of Burnt-sugar Syrup.

Burnt-sugar Syrup

　Melt (caramelize) ⅔ cup sugar in large heavy skillet, stirring constantly—careful, it's *hot*! When a dark brown syrup, remove from heat; slowly add ⅔ cup boiling water. Heat and stir till all dissolves.

　Boil to reduce syrup to ½ cup—this is enough for both cake and frosting. *Cool* syrup before using.

Date Filling

　Combine 1½ cups dates, cut up, ⅓ cup sugar, 1 cup water, and ¼ teaspoon salt; bring to boiling. Cook gently, stirring constantly, about 4 minutes or till thick. Remove from heat. Cool to room temperature.

　Fold in ¼ cup Burnt-sugar Frosting (not syrup) and ¼ cup chopped California walnuts. Spread between thoroughly cooled cake layers. Makes about 1½ cups.

Lovely table to honor a favorite friend or aunt. Little gifts add a pretty accent!

Holidays, *family*

style!

When friends and family gather, you want the food positively wonderful! You'll appreciate this chapter of good recipes all year round!

New Year's Eve...
teens entertain

Ring in the New Year with a Burger-que! On the next page is a roundup of recipes to make putting on a party no trick at all! Invite the gang, and get set for fun and fabulous food!

Time out for refreshments! Little grill broils burgers—each person chefs his own (that's part of the fun!) and stacks his sandwich with all the fixings!

For dessert, spin the Lazy Susan to your favorite version of an Ad-infinitum Sundae.

Make-your-own Party

Ad-lib Burgers *or*
Sloppy Joes *or*
Coney Islands
Mustard, Pickle Relish,
Hamburger Relish, Catsup
Grated Cheese, Chopped Onion,
Cucumber Slices, Tomato Slices
Potato Chips   Creamy Onion Dip
Ad-infinitum Sundaes
Chilled Pop

It's party time!

On with the records—and on with the food for a big New Year's Eve at home! Here are your favorite foods, but not ordinary hamburgers or franks and everyday sundaes. These are nothing short of fantabulous, just right to welcome the New Year (but you needn't wait till then).

The big idea is for the gang to concoct their own burgers or coneys. Set out all the makings for easy pick-up: Sizzling burgers or frankfurters and soft, buttery buns. Line up the mustard, pickle relish, hamburger relish, and catsup. And don't forget the cheese, onion, tomato, and cucumber slices.

To give you an assist, you can't do better than the little tote grill that's plugged in by the table—see picture, page 28. It lets you, the cook or chef, stay with the party. Roll it in on a handy cart—have a tray of meat patties ready for broiling on the shelf underneath. You'll be all set for cooking those second orders!

When it's time for dessert, give a Lazy Susan of Ad-infinitum Sundaes a turn. Circle a half dozen or more sauces and toppings around a fruit centerpiece (just unzip those bananas as needed for splits).

For real cool serving of your ice-cream buffet, bed down a trio of cartons in chipped ice. Line a basket-holder with aluminum foil, or use a large bowl.

For simple neat cleanup, use paper plates and cups. Now for the recipes. We guarantee they'll make a big hit!

Ad-lib Burgers

1 pound hamburger
¼ cup finely chopped onion
1 tablespoon bottled steak sauce
1 teaspoon prepared mustard
1 teaspoon salt
Dash pepper

• • •

4 slices American cheese
4 hamburger buns, split, heated,
    and buttered
Fixings for ad-libbing

Mix the first 6 ingredients well. Shape in 4 patties, about ¼ to ½ inch thick. Broil 3 inches from heat for 6 minutes; turn and broil 4 minutes longer or till done "your way." Top each with cheese last minute of broiling so it'll be melty. Slide burgers into hot buttered buns.

Now to ad-lib: Add some or all of the fixings shown (see page 28), or pile on what-have-you. To hold sandwich together, tack with a green onion on a toothpick. Makes 4 servings.

Sloppy Joes

1 pound ground beef
1½ cups chopped onion
1½ cups chopped celery

• • •

1 can condensed tomato soup
½ cup extra-hot catsup
1 teaspoon salt
1 teaspoon monosodium glutamate
Dash pepper
5 or 6 hamburger buns, split and
    toasted

Brown ground beef. Add onion and celery; cook until tender but not brown. Add soup, catsup, and seasonings. Simmer uncovered about 20 minutes or until of the consistency you like. Salt to taste.

Spoon between or over toasted bun halves. Makes 5 or 6 servings.

Coney Islands

Place 1½ pounds (about 12) franks in boiling water; reduce heat and simmer (don't boil) 5 to 8 minutes. Set everything out, help-yourself style; let folks pop franks in heated coney buns, smear on prepared mustard, spoon on chopped onion, then hot Coney Sauce. Makes 12 Coneys.

Coney Sauce

Tune this in next time you have hot dogs. Good? It's the most!—

½ pound ground beef

• • •

¼ cup water
¼ cup chopped onion
1 clove garlic, minced
1 8-ounce can (1 cup) seasoned tomato
    sauce
½ to ¾ teaspoon chili powder
½ teaspoon monosodium glutamate
½ teaspoon salt

Brown ground beef slowly but thoroughly, breaking with a fork till fine. Add remaining ingredients; simmer uncovered 10 minutes. Serve in bowl to ladle over *hot* franks in *heated* coney buns. Makes enough sauce for 12 Coney Islands.

Creamy Onion Dip

Blend 1½ cups dairy sour cream and 2 tablespoons packaged onion-soup mix. Stir in 2 ounces blue cheese (crumbled), and ⅓ cup chopped California walnuts. Serve with potato chips. Makes 2 cups.

Ad-infinitum Sundaes

Here's a chance to be your own soda jerk—

Ice creams—maybe three, like
    chocolate
    vanilla
    strawberry
Sundae gooperoos, like
    fudge sauce
    marshmallow creme
    butterscotch topping
    date-nut topping
Crowning glories, like
    whipped cream
    maraschino cherries
    walnut halves
Go-alongs, like
    crisp vanilla wafers
    filled cookies

Start each sundae with a couple spoonfuls of sauce or topping. Scoop in your choice of ice creams. Drizzle with sauces or toppings till you flood the dish. Cap with whipped cream, nuts, etc. Eat with cookies.

Uptown Pineapple Sauce

1 9-ounce can (1 cup) pineapple
    tidbits
½ cup light corn syrup
¼ teaspoon mint extract
2 drops green food coloring

Combine ingredients, mixing well. Chill. Makes 1½ cups sauce.

Date-Nut Sundae Topping

½ cup sliced pitted dates
½ cup dark corn syrup
¼ cup brown sugar
¼ cup water
Dash salt
½ teaspoon vanilla
½ cup chopped California walnuts
    or pecans

Combine dates, corn syrup, brown sugar, water, and salt in a saucepan. Bring to boiling, and cook 2 minutes over medium heat, stirring constantly.

Remove from heat; add vanilla and nuts. Mix well. Cool; serve over vanilla ice cream. Makes 4 to 6 servings.

Gooey Fudge Sauce

1 6-ounce package (1 cup) semisweet
    chocolate pieces
½ cup evaporated milk

In small heavy saucepan, heat chocolate and evaporated milk over medium heat, stirring constantly till blended. Serve warm or at room temperature over ice cream. Makes 1 cup.

Easy Caramel Topping

Combine ½ pound (28) caramels with ½ cup hot water in top of double boiler. Heat over hot water, stirring occasionally till caramels melt. Serve warm or cool over ice cream. Makes 1 cup sauce.

Raspberry Sundae Topping

Thaw and crush one 10-ounce package frozen red raspberries. Combine with 1½ teaspoons cornstarch; add ½ cup currant jelly. Bring to boiling. Cook and stir until clear and slightly thick. Strain and cool.

When St. Valentine's Day rolls around, call on these salad beauties to lend a happy note. It's a delicious way to say "Be mine!" Or choose a colorful Cherry Meringue Torte or gay polka-dot cupcakes to highlight your February refreshments.

Hearts and flowers trim the dinner table

The Valentine Ring-around Salad (at right) is a luscious combination of cheese, grapes, pecans, and chive snippets. Salad Hearts (above) are rich, creamy molds dotted with fruit cocktail and tiny marshmallow fluffs. Center tray with *Fluffy Pink Mayonnaise:* Whip ½ cup whipping cream; fold in 1 cup of mayonnaise. Fold in a drop or so of red food coloring to tint a delicate pink.

Please be my valentine!

Hearts-and-Flowers Fare!

Heart Sandwiches with Ham Salad Filling
Cherry Tomatoes   Celery Hearts
Salad Hearts atop Pineapple Rings
with Fluffy Pink Mayonnaise *or*
Valentine Ring-around Salad
with Green Grapes
Pink Mints
Hot Tea

Salad Hearts

1 No. 2½ can (3½ cups) fruit cocktail
1 package lemon-flavored gelatin
1 cup hot water
¼ cup maraschino-cherry syrup
2 tablespoons lemon juice

• • •

2 3-ounce packages cream cheese
½ cup mayonnaise or salad dressing
1½ cups tiny marshmallows
¼ cup quartered maraschino cherries
1 cup whipping cream, whipped
Few drops red food coloring

Drain fruit cocktail, reserving 1 cup syrup. Dissolve gelatin in hot water; add reserved fruit-cocktail syrup, maraschino-cherry syrup, and lemon juice. Chill till partially set. Soften cream cheese; add mayonnaise and beat till smooth. Add to gelatin mixture, mixing well. Stir in fruit cocktail, marshmallows, and cherries. Fold in whipped cream. Tint pink with red food coloring. Pour into individual heart molds.*

Freeze salad several hours or overnight. Unmold atop canned pineapple rings. If desired, top with Gelatin Heart Cutouts. Makes 12 large or 18 small servings.

*Freeze any extra in refrigerator tray.

Valentine Ring-around

Mash together one 12-ounce carton (1½ cups) cream-style cottage cheese and two 3-ounce packages cream cheese till well blended. Soften 1 *teaspoon* unflavored gelatin in ¼ cup cold water; dissolve over hot water; add ¼ teaspoon salt. Stir gelatin mixture into cheese mixture.

Add 1 cup seedless green grapes, ½ cup broken pecans, 2 tablespoons chopped chives. Fold in 1 cup whipping cream, whipped. Turn into 5-cup ring mold or individual molds. Chill till firm. Unmold. Top with Gelatin Heart Cutouts. Makes 6 to 8 servings.

Note: To serve larger groups, double this recipe. Use a 2-quart ring mold.

Gelatin Heart Cutouts

Dissolve one package cherry- *or* strawberry- *or* raspberry-flavored gelatin in 2 cups hot water. Pour into shallow baking dish—gelatin should be a little less than ½ inch deep. Chill firm. Cut out hearts with cooky cutter. To remove the first cutout, slit a piece of gelatin between designs and pull out scraps; lift the cutout with spatula. Serve atop Valentine salads.

Make Heart Sandwiches with cooky cutters and both white and dark bread

Cut large hearts, circles, and 2-inch squares from both white and dark bread. (If you freeze the bread and cut while frozen, edges won't crush.)

Cut small hearts in the center of half the cutouts of each color—if you have tiny heart hors d'oeuvre cutters, cut twin hearts.

To make the inlaid sandwich tops, replace the small cutout hearts in the white bread with ones of dark bread, and vice versa.

Spread the plain bases with your choice of sandwich filling. You may want to use egg salad, ham salad, or process cheese spread. Top filling with an "inlaid" cutout of the same shape, but of contrasting color.

Children's Valentine Party

Queen-of-Hearts Cupcakes
Valentine Candies
Red-and-White Sundaes
Cold Milk

Valentine Invitations

Cut 6-inch hearts out of red drawing paper. Separate each into two parts for a "broken heart"—cut jaggedly from indentation at top down to tip. No two hearts should be cut apart exactly the same.

On each half-heart, write your invitation, plus the admonition, "Bring this broken heart to find your Secret Pal." Guests will enjoy fitting the edges to find the matching half.

Queen-of-Hearts Frosting

1 egg white
¾ cup sugar
2 tablespoons heart-shaped red
  cinnamon candies
Dash salt
½ cup applesauce
1 teaspoon light corn syrup

Combine all ingredients in top of double boiler. Beat 1 minute with electric or rotary beater. Place over boiling water; beat constantly until mixture forms peaks, *about* 4 minutes. (Careful—don't overcook!) Remove from boiling water.

Beat until of spreading consistency, about 2 minutes. Frosts tops of 12 cupcakes or tops and sides of one 9-inch square cake. Dot with additional red candies.

Red-and-White Sundaes

Place tiny scoops of vanilla ice cream in dessert dishes. Top with red-raspberry preserves or Quick Cherry Sauce.

Quick Cherry Sauce: Chop drained maraschino cherries. Add light corn syrup and a little lemon juice to taste; add a dash of salt. Spoon over ice cream.

Cherry Meringue Torte— nice for a February party!

Shell: Beat 3 egg whites with 1 teaspoon vanilla and dash salt till foamy. Gradually add 1 cup sugar; beat to stiff peaks. Mix ¾ cup chopped walnuts, ½ cup saltine-cracker crumbs, and 1 teaspoon baking powder; fold into egg whites. Spread in well-greased 9-inch pie plate, building up sides. Bake at 300° about 40 minutes. Cool.

Filling: Drain 1 No. 2 can (2½ cups) frozen pitted tart red cherries, reserving syrup. Combine ¾ *cup syrup* and ¼ cup sugar; heat to boiling. Add cherries; cook 10 minutes. Mix 2 tablespoons cornstarch with remaining cold syrup; add to hot mixture. Cook, stirring constantly, till thick and clear. Cool. Whip 1 cup whipping cream; line Shell with *half.* Fill with cherry mixture; top with remaining cream.

Festive for Easter

Roast Leg of Lamb

Without removing the fell (paperlike covering), season leg of lamb with salt and pepper. Place meat fat side up on rack in shallow roasting pan. Do not cover; do not add water. Roast in slow oven (325°) until meat thermometer reads 170° to 175° (allow about 30 to 35 minutes per pound).

Let roast stand about 10 minutes to firm before carving. Count on 2 to 3 servings per pound. Trim with sprigs of mint, serve with Fresh Mint Sauce.

Cake Nests with jellybean eggs

The nests can be spongecake cups from the store or rounds cut out of a sheet cake with a big cooky cutter. All you do is coat cake rounds with 7-minute Frosting, sprinkle with green coconut, fill with candy eggs. To tint coconut, place shredded or flaked coconut in a jar. Add a few drops of green food coloring. Screw on lid; shake till coconut is uniformly colored.

Fresh Mint Sauce

¼ cup sugar
½ cup vinegar
¼ cup water
Dash salt
½ cup finely snipped mint leaves

Combine sugar, vinegar, water and salt. Bring to boiling, reduce heat and simmer uncovered 5 minutes. Pour immediately over mint; let stand 30 minutes to steep.

Serve as is or strain. Offer hot or chilled with roast lamb. Makes ½ cup sauce.

Herbed Carrots

2 tablespoons butter or margarine
2 tablespoons water
1 teaspoon sugar
4 cups quartered carrots
Salt and white pepper to taste
1 teaspoon snipped parsley
1 teaspoon snipped fresh tarragon
  or ¼ teaspoon dried whole
  tarragon, crushed

In heavy saucepan, combine butter, water, and sugar; add carrots. Cover tightly and cook gently over *low* heat 15 to 20 minutes or till done. Add salt and pepper; sprinkle with parsley and tarragon. Serve without draining. Makes 6 servings.

Creamed Peas and New Potatoes

Scrub 1½ pounds (about 15) tiny new potatoes; pare off narrow strip of peel around center of each. Cook in boiling salted water till done, about 15 to 20 minutes; drain thoroughly.

Meanwhile, cook 1 to 1½ pounds fresh peas, shelled, and 3 tablespoons finely sliced green onion in small amount boiling salted water 8 to 15 minutes; drain.

Make white sauce of 4 teaspoons *each* butter and flour, dash salt, and 1 cup milk. Combine hot vegetables and pour sauce over. Makes 4 to 6 servings.

Frozen Orange-Pecan Molds

A rich, fruity make-ahead salad. Top with mayonnaise, trim with maraschino cherry—

> 1 8-ounce package cream cheese, softened
> ¼ cup orange juice
> ½ cup chopped pecans
> 1 9-ounce can (1 cup) crushed pineapple, drained
> ½ cup pitted dates, cut up
> ¼ cup chopped maraschino cherries
> ½ teaspoon grated orange peel
>
> • • •
>
> 1 cup whipping cream, whipped

Combine cheese and orange juice, beating till fluffy. Stir in pecans and fruits. Fold in whipped cream. *Pack* into individual molds or into 8½x4½x2½-inch loaf pan. Freeze firm; let stand at room temperature about 15 minutes before serving. For a boost in height, unmold salads on orange slices. Makes 8 servings.

Yes, very fancy for Easter eggs

Get a head start with ready-made decorations from variety or display store. First, tint the eggshells (hard-cooked eggs or blown eggshells) with food coloring or special egg dye.

Here, butterfly hovers over paper pompon posy. (Both are the inexpensive dime-store kind.) Now, let your imagination take over!

Spooks and
...tonight is

Popcorn Balls

This recipe is really two in one! You can use same syrup with puffed rice cereal—

> 5 quarts popped corn
> 2 cups sugar
> 1½ cups water
> ½ teaspoon salt
> ½ cup light corn syrup
> 1 teaspoon vinegar
> 1 teaspoon vanilla

Keep popped corn hot and crisp in slow oven (300° to 325°). Butter sides of saucepan. In it combine sugar, water, salt, corn syrup, and vinegar. Cook to hard-ball stage (250°). Add vanilla. Pour slowly over hot popped corn, stirring just enough to mix thoroughly. Lightly butter hands before shaping into balls or flat circles.

Caramel Popcorn Balls

> 2½ quarts popped corn
> ½ pound (28) vanilla caramels
> 2 tablespoons water

Keep popped corn hot and crisp in slow oven (300 to 325°). Melt caramels in 2 tablespoons water in a double boiler, stirring frequently. Add dash salt. Place popped corn in large bowl and drizzle caramel sauce over; toss till corn is well coated. Butter hands and shape in balls.

Marshmallow Stickum

Just right for holding candies in place. See funny faces, page 41—

Melt ⅔ cup tiny marshmallows (or 6 big ones) with 2 teaspoons shortening over low heat. Use mixture while warm. Dip candies in Stickum, pop them onto faces.

witches will be coming Halloween!

Best-ever Candy Corn

2½ quarts popped corn
1 pound (2¼ cups) light brown sugar
½ cup light corn syrup
½ cup water
½ cup butter or margarine
2 teaspoons salt
1 tablespoon vanilla
1 cup salted peanuts

Keep popped corn hot and crisp in slow oven (300° to 325°). In large saucepan, combine sugar, syrup, water, butter, and salt. Cook over moderate heat, stirring occasionally, until syrup reaches hard crack stage (290°). Remove from heat, stir in vanilla. In large buttered bowl or pan, mix nuts and popcorn. Pour syrup in fine stream over mixture.

Working quickly, mix well until kernels are completely coated. Spread out thin on buttered cooky sheets. Quickly separate into bite-size clusters with 2 buttered forks. Cool. Makes about 3½ quarts.

Caramel Apples

1 pound (56) vanilla caramels
2 tablespoons water
Dash salt
6 wooden skewers
6 crisp, medium apples
Chopped California walnuts

Melt caramels with water in double boiler, stirring frequently until smooth. Add salt. Stick a skewer into blossom end of each apple. Dip apple in the caramel syrup and turn until surface is completely coated. (If syrup is too stiff, add few drops water.) At once roll bottom half of coated apple in chopped nuts. Set on cooky sheet covered with waxed paper. Chill in refrigerator until firm. Makes 6 servings.

Spooky Cupcakes with masks

Witch's Pussycat: For ears bend hollow licorice twists; insert one end of toothpick in hollow, other end in cake. Eyes are a black jellybean, halved lengthwise. Add red gumdrop nose, licorice strips for whiskers.

Hooty Owl: Eye outlines are "peel" cut from two orange jellied fruit slices. His owlish eyes are orange pumpkin candies; snip of candy orange slice makes beak.

Little Good Witch: Use licorice twist for hat and curls. (Make hat crown like cat's ears, but larger.) Add bit of jellied fruit slice for mouth, halved licorice drop for eyes, a candy-coated licorice stick for nose.

When little ghosts come a-knocking, greet them with handouts like these!

A trick for Dad—treat the kids! Dad quickly carves wide eyes and a toothy smile, and the knife work is done on this unique jack-o'-lantern. Then it's up to the kids (using toothpicks and hairpins) to fit him out with a carrot nose, green-pepper ears, olive eyes, and bushy parsley brows.

For the funny faces, Mother contributes Popcorn Balls (recipe, page 38). Halloween candy makes the rest easy!

Chief Jellybean. One recipe Popcorn Balls (page 38) makes 12 Chiefs. Place a 3½x1-inch circle mold* on a greased cooky sheet; press the mixture into mold. Remove mold and insert end of wooden skewer in the edge of popcorn round.

Attach Chief's features with Marshmallow Stickum (page 38). A piece of giant candy corn has just the right angles for Indian's nose. Add jellybean eyes, bits of a jellied fruit slice for mouth and war paint. For feather headdress, slip jelly strings on toothpicks and poke around the edge; add headband of little gumdrops. Slip a wide, flat gumdrop on skewer and push up under Chief's chin. Anchor skewer in big apple.

*For mold, cut cardboard strip, 4 inches long and 1 inch wide; cover with aluminum foil. Fasten ends of strip together with paper clip to make a 3½-inch circle.

Good Witch Curlilocks. Prepare one recipe Popcorn Balls, (recipe, page 38), shaping in six or seven 4-inch balls. Attach curls of licorice whips with toothpicks. Snip off one end of a purple jelly-string for a nose and curve it down—that can give witch a really dour look! Marshmallow Stickum (recipe, page 38) comes to the rescue and holds both nose and licorice-drop eyes in place. Licorice-strip mouth is fastened at the corners with toothpicks.

Witch's hat: Make a black-paper circle 12 inches in diameter; cut in half (each circle makes the peaked crowns for 2 hats). Roll each half-circle into a cone that is 3 inches in diameter at the bottom; fasten with cellophane tape or staples. For hat brim cut a 5½-inch circle from black paper; out of the center cut another circle, 3 inches across. Perch the hat crown on the popcorn ball, then slip the brim over the top.

For a base for Witch Curlilocks, use an inverted paper cup with the bottom removed. Her bowknot is made from a licorice whip, attached to the cup with pins.

Peter Pumpkin Eater. From Caramel Popcorn mixture (recipe, page 38), shape three or four 3½- to 4-inch balls. With Marshmallow Stickum (recipe, page 38), add orange pumpkin candies for eyes. Wide smile is a licorice strip anchored at the corners with toothpicks. Black jellybean slipped on a toothpick and poked into popcorn ball becomes a snub nose. Insert a piece of licorice whip at top of pumpkin for a stem.

Thomas Candy Cat. Heat 3½ quarts puffed rice cereal in moderate oven (350°) 10 minutes to crisp. Prepare syrup as directed for Popcorn Balls (page 38), and pour over the hot cereal. Quickly shape in seven 3½- to 4-inch balls.

Add perky ears made from hollow licorice strips—bend to shape, and insert one end of toothpick in hollow to hold erect, other end in cereal ball. Whiskers are colored toothpicks. For cat's eyes, use striped black anise balls. Balance Tom Cat on a paper nut cup. Complete him by adding a licorice nose and jellied-fruit-slice bow tie with Marshmallow Stickum.

Thanksgiving dinner

Traditional recipes as lovingly cooked by mothers and grandmothers down through the years—they'll bring to your kitchen the fragrances and cheerful hum of Thanksgiving cooking—to your family, glorious feasting!

Family Dinner

Tomato Starter—hot or cold
Curried Wheat Bites
Roast Turkey Corn-bread Stuffing
Cranberry Jelly Mold
Mashed Potatoes
Green Beans Almond
Classic Waldorf Salad
Melon Pickles   Assorted Olives
Cloverleaf Rolls
Mince Pie   Hard Sauce
Hot Coffee

Here's unusual and good nibbling for early-to-arrive guests.

Curried Wheat Bites: Melt ⅓ cup butter in large skillet. Blend in ½ teaspoon curry powder, ¼ teaspoon onion salt, and ⅛ teaspoon ginger.

Add 3 cups (about 25) spoon-size shredded-wheat biscuits and toss to butter. Heat about 5 minutes over low heat, stirring frequently. Drain on paper towels. Serve warm.

Tomato Starter—Hot

1 46-ounce can (about 6 cups)
   tomato juice
1 can condensed consomme
1 teaspoon grated onion
1 teaspoon prepared horseradish
Dash pepper
1 teaspoon Worcestershire sauce
• • •
1 lemon, sliced
Whole cloves

In saucepan, combine juice, consomme, onion, horseradish, pepper, and Worcestershire. Stud lemon slices with cloves; add to juice and heat just to boiling. Serve immediately, with lemon slices as floaters in each cup. Makes 8 to 10 servings.

Tomato Starter—Cold

1 No. 2 can (2¼ cups) tomato juice
3 tablespoons lemon juice
1 teaspoon sugar
¼ teaspoon celery salt
1 teaspoon Worcestershire sauce

Combine all ingredients and chill. Stir before serving. Makes 4 or 5 servings.

Roast Stuffed Turkey

Stuff and truss: Stuff turkey just before roasting. Allow ¾ cup stuffing per pound ready-to-cook weight. Rinse bird; pat dry with paper towels. Stuff wishbone cavity and skewer neck skin to back. Tuck wing tips behind shoulder joints. Rub large cavity with salt.

Spoon in stuffing. Shake bird to settle stuffing; do not pack. Close opening by placing skewers across it and lacing shut with cord. Tie drumsticks securely to tail. (If opening has band of skin across, push drumsticks underneath, and you won't need to fasten opening or tie legs.)

Grease skin thoroughly. Insert meat thermometer in center of the inside thigh muscle adjoining the cavity.

To roast: Place bird breast up on rack (put breast down if using V-rack) in shallow roasting pan and leave in this position for entire roasting time. Cover with loose "cap" of aluminum foil, pressing it lightly at drumstick and breast ends, but *avoid having it touch top or sides.* Roast at constant *low* temperature (see chart).

When turkey is about two-thirds done, according to chart, cut cord or band of skin so heat can reach inside of thighs.

Doneness tests: About 20 minutes before roasting time is up, test doneness by pressing thick part of drumstick between fingers (protect hand with paper towel). Meat should feel very soft. Move drumstick up and down; it should move easily or twist out of joint. (Meat thermometer should register 195°.) When done, remove from pan and keep warm while you make gravy from drippings. Let stand 20 minutes to firm before carving.

Corn-bread Stuffing

Toss together 3 cups slightly dry bread cubes, 5 cups coarsely crumbled corn bread, 1 teaspoon poultry seasoning, 1 teaspoon salt, and dash pepper. Cook 1 cup finely chopped celery and ½ cup finely chopped onion in ½ cup butter or margarine till tender but not brown; pour over bread.

Add 2 beaten eggs and toss lightly to mix. Moisten with ¼ cup chicken broth or water, and toss to mix. Makes enough stuffing for a 10-pound turkey.

Turkey roasting chart

Set oven at 325°. Times are for chilled turkeys, stuffed just before roasting, and are approximate only.

Ready-to-cook weight (before stuffing)	Time (total)
6 to 8 lbs.	3½ to 4 hrs.
8 to 12 lbs.	4 to 4½ hrs.
12 to 16 lbs.	4½ to 5½ hrs.
16 to 20 lbs.	5½ to 7 hrs.
20 to 24 lbs.	7 to 8½ hrs.

Foil-wrapped roasting chart

Set over at 450°. Times are for unstuffed chilled turkeys and are approximate only. For stuffed turkey, add 30 to 45 minutes to the total roasting time.

Ready-to-cook weight (before stuffing)	Time (total)
8 to 10 lbs.	2¼ to 2½ hrs.
10 to 12 lbs.	2¾ to 3 hrs.
14 to 16 lbs.	3 to 3¼ hrs.
18 to 20 lbs.	3¼ to 3½ hrs.
22 to 24 lbs.	3¼ to 3¾ hrs.

What turkey figure is for you?

Turkey Size	Servings
4 to 8 lbs.	4 to 10
8 to 12 lbs.	10 to 20
12 to 16 lbs.	20 to 30
16 to 20 lbs.	30 to 40
20 to 24 lbs.	40 to 50

Foil-wrapped Roast Turkey

To wrap: Use heavy, wide aluminum foil. Place trussed turkey, breast up, in center of foil. (Foil should be wide enough to have 5 to 6 inches extending beyond leg and breast ends of bird; if it isn't join 2 pieces together with drugstore or lock fold, pressing to make leakproof joining. To prevent puncturing, wrap small folds of foil around tips of drumsticks and wings.)

Grease skin. Bring one end of foil snugly over top of turkey; bring opposite end up, lapping over first (overlap should be 2 to 3 inches). Now fold foil down snugly at breast and legs; then press remaining two sides of foil up (foil should come up high enough to prevent drippings from running into the pan and burning).

To roast: Place foil-wrapped bird, breast up, in bottom of shallow pan (broiler pan is convenient)—do not use rack. Roast at constant, *high temperature.* (See Foil-wrapped-turkey roasting chart.)

When turkey has cooked to within *15 to 20 minutes of total cooking time* given in the foil-wrapped-turkey roasting chart, open foil for browning. Continue roasting till turkey is tender (test doneness in usual ways). When turkey's done, lift from foil to warm platter. Use the pan drippings in making gravy.

Frozen Turkeys (*stuffed*)

All you do is unwrap and roast the turkey. (And stew the giblets, of course.) *Keep turkey frozen* until you are ready to cook it —however, you may transfer turkey from freezer to refrigerator the night before cooking; this cuts roasting time by about 1 hour. *Follow to the letter, the directions that come with the bird.*

Frozen Turkeys (*unstuffed*)

Thaw frozen unstuffed turkey in the original wrapping shortly before time to cook. To thaw a 12- to 20-pound turkey (ready-to-cook weight), allow 2 to 3 days in the refrigerator at 40°. To speed up thawing, you can place wrapped turkey under cold running water. See the label directions that come with the turkey.

Cranberry Jelly Mold

2 pounds (8 cups) cranberries
4 cups water
4 cups sugar

Cook cranberries in water until skins pop, about 3 to 5 minutes. Put through sieve or food mill. Stir in sugar. Boil rapidly 10 to 15 minutes, or until a drop jells on a chilled plate. Skim off foam. Pour into a 1½-quart mold; chill until firm, about 5 hours. Unmold on platter.

Classic Waldorf Salad

Sprinkle 2 cups diced tart apples with 1 tablespoon sugar, ½ teaspoon lemon juice, and dash salt. Add 1 cup 1-inch julienne celery sticks and ½ cup broken walnuts.

Fold ¼ cup mayonnaise into ½ cup whipping cream, whipped. Gently fold into apple mixture. Chill. Makes 6 servings.

Mince Pie

1¾ cups prepared mincemeat
  or 1 9-ounce package
2 cups thinly sliced apples
½ teaspoon grated lemon peel
2 tablespoons lemon juice
Pastry for 2-crust 8-inch pie

If using packaged mincemeat, prepare according to label directions. Combine mincemeat with apples, lemon peel, and lemon juice. Line 8-inch pie plate with pastry; fill. Adjust top crust and crimp edges.

With cooky cutter or knife, cut design in crust. Sprinkle lightly with sugar for sparkle. Bake in hot oven (400°) about 35 minutes. Serve while warm.

Hard Sauce

Thoroughly cream ½ cup butter or margarine and 2 cups sifted confectioners' sugar. Add 1 teaspoon vanilla. (Vary flavor with lemon or orange juice and shredded peel.) Spread in an 8x8x2-inch pan; chill to harden. With small cooky cutter, cut in shapes, or cut squares. Makes 1⅓ cups.

Fluffy Hard Sauce: Add 1 egg yolk to creamed mixture in recipe above. Last, fold in one stiff-beaten egg white. Chill.

Turkey Dinner, No Carving

Spiced Orange Toddy
Turkey Pieces   Candied Sweets
Broccoli   Jiffy Hollandaise
Cranberry-Apple Delight
or
Jellied Cranberry Slices
Brown-and-serve Rolls
Pumpkin Tarts   Coffee

Spiced Orange Toddy

Delightful! Flavored just right—

4 cups orange juice
⅛ to ½ cup sugar
6 inches stick cinnamon
2 teaspoons whole cloves
2 teaspoons grated orange peel

Combine all ingredients in saucepan. Bring to boiling, then simmer 5 minutes. Strain. Serve hot. Float orange slices atop, if desired. Makes about 8 servings.

Jiffy Hollandaise

½ cup salad dressing or mayonnaise
2 teaspoons prepared mustard
1 teaspoon lemon juice

Combine ingredients. Heat over low heat, stirring constantly till heated through. (Do not boil.) Serve over hot cooked broccoli spears. Makes ½ cup sauce.

Cranberry-Apple Delight

1 3-ounce package raspberry-flavored gelatin
1¼ cups boiling water
1 1-pound can (2 cups) whole cranberry sauce

• • •

1 cup diced unpared tart red apple
½ cup finely chopped celery
¼ cup broken California walnuts

Dissolve gelatin in hot water. Add cranberry sauce; chill till partially set. Add remaining ingredients. Pour into 7 or 8 individual molds or a 4-cup mold. Chill till firm.

Unmold on greens. Serve with mayonnaise. Makes 6 to 8 servings.

Feast for a foursome!

A young family, just getting settled, will appreciate the idea of dinner a la card table. Also the turkey pieces that need no carving, the easy but festive recipes.

Pumpkin Tarts

1½ cups canned pumpkin
¾ cup sugar
½ teaspoon salt
1 to 1¼ teaspoons cinnamon
½ to 1 teaspoon ginger
¼ to ½ teaspoon nutmeg
¼ to ½ teaspoon cloves
3 slightly beaten eggs
1¼ cups milk
1 6-ounce can (⅔ cup) evaporated milk
1 recipe Plain Pastry for Tarts

Thoroughly combine pumpkin, sugar, salt, and spices. Blend in eggs, milk, and evaporated milk. Pour into 8 unbaked 3½-inch tart shells (have edges crimped high).

Bake in hot oven (400°) 35 minutes, or until knife inserted halfway between center and edge comes out clean. Cool.

Pumpkin Tarts—a pretty, individualized version of the traditional Thanksgiving pie. And don't forget cup after cup of coffee!

Plain Pastry for Tarts

2½ cups sifted all-purpose flour
1 teaspoon salt
¾ cup shortening
6 to 8 tablespoons cold water

Sift together flour and salt; cut in shortening with pastry blender or blending fork till pieces are the size of small peas.

Sprinkle 1 tablespoon of the water over part of mixture. Gently toss with fork; push to side of bowl. Sprinkle next tablespoon water over dry part; mix lightly; push to moistened part at side. Repeat till all is moistened. Form in ball.

Divide dough in quarters; then divide each quarter in half; shape in balls. Flatten each ball slightly and roll ⅛ inch thick on slightly floured surface. Fit into tart pans. Crimp edges high. Makes pastry for eight 3½-inch tart shells.

Candied Sweets

Melt 2 tablespoons butter or margarine and ⅓ cup orange marmalade in skillet. Add one 18-ounce can whole yams or sweet potatoes, drained. Dash with salt.

Heat, uncovered, over low heat about 5 minutes, basting often till potatoes are glazed and hot through. (If necessary, add 1 tablespoon water or liquid from potatoes, while heating.) Makes 5 or 6 servings.

Fried Turkey Pieces

½ cup all-purpose flour
2 teaspoons salt
2 teaspoons paprika
¼ teaspoon pepper
1 fryer-roaster turkey,* 3½ to 6 pounds, ready-to-cook weight, cut in pieces

Combine flour and seasonings. Rub into turkey pieces. Place on rack to let coating dry. Heat fat (½ inch deep in large skillet) till it will sizzle a drop of water. Brown only a few turkey pieces at a time—don't crowd. Brown one side slowly; turn—use tongs so not to pierce. When first pieces are brown, remove and set aside while you brown the next lot; return all to skillet. Or use two large skillets.

When lightly browned, 15 to 20 minutes, reduce heat; cover. (If cover is not tight, add 1 to 2 tablespoons water.) Cook until tender, about 1 hour. Uncover last 10 minutes to crisp. Makes 6 to 8 servings.

*If turkey is frozen, thaw completely in refrigerator (you'll need to allow 1 to 2 days) before cooking.

Oven-cooked Turkey Pieces: Coat turkey and brown as for Fried Turkey Pieces. Add ¼ to ⅓ cup milk to lightly browned turkey in oven-going skillet or casserole. Cover tightly and bake in slow oven (325°) 1¼ to 1½ hours or till fork-tender. Uncover last 15 to 20 minutes to crisp.

Sugarplum sweets...
for keeping Christmas

You'll catch
the holiday
spirit with these
merry favorites—
cookies, candies,
popcorn balls,
fruit-filled bread.

Gingerbread Boys

1 cup shortening
1 cup sugar
½ teaspoon salt
1 egg
1 cup molasses
2 tablespoons vinegar

    •   •   •

5 cups sifted all-purpose flour
1½ teaspoons soda
1 tablespoon ginger
1 teaspoon cinnamon
1 teaspoon ground cloves

Thoroughly cream shortening, sugar, and salt. Stir in egg, molasses, and vinegar; beat well. Sift dry ingredients; stir into molasses mixture. Chill (about 3 hours). On lightly floured surface, roll to ⅛ inch. Cut with gingerbread-boy cutter.

Place 1 inch apart on greased cooky sheet. Use red hots for faces and buttons. Bake in moderate oven (375°) about 6 minutes. Cool slightly; remove to rack. When thoroughly cool, decorate with Confectioners' Icing. Makes about 5 dozen.

Confectioners' Icing

Add sufficient light cream or half-and-half to 2 cups confectioners' sugar to make of the consistency you need. For piped trim (Gingerbread Boys) add only enough liquid to make a mixture that will go through a pastry tube easily and hold its shape. For bread glaze, make icing a little thinner than spreading consistency. For cooky glaze, have it runny.

Quick Almond Crunch

In heavy skillet, melt 1 cup butter; stir in 1 cup sugar. Add 1½ cups slivered blanched almonds, stir constantly over medium heat till mixture is golden brown (about 10 to 15 minutes).

Pour into jelly roll pan, spreading thinly. Immediately sprinkle with ½ to 1 cup semisweet chocolate pieces; spread evenly to glaze. Chill.

When chocolate is set, crack candy into pieces. Store in covered container in the refrigerator.

Grandma's Fudge

2 cups sugar
¾ cup milk
2 1-ounce squares unsweetened
    chocolate
1 teaspoon corn syrup, light or dark
2 tablespoons butter or margarine
1 teaspoon vanilla

Butter sides of heavy 2-quart saucepan. In it combine sugar, milk, chocolate, dash salt, and corn syrup. Heat over medium heat, stirring constantly till sugar dissolves, chocolate melts, and mixture comes to boiling. Then cook to soft-ball stage (234°), stirring only if necessary.

Immediately remove from heat; add butter; cool to lukewarm (110°) without stirring. Add vanilla. Beat vigorously till fudge becomes very thick and starts to lose its gloss. Quickly spread in buttered shallow pans or small platter. Score in squares while warm, cut when firm.

Note: If you like, quickly stir in ½ cup broken walnuts at end of beating time.

German Lebkuchen

Beat 1 egg; add ¾ cup brown sugar and beat till fluffy. Stir in ½ cup *each* honey and dark molasses. Sift together 3 cups sifted all-purpose flour, 1¼ teaspoons *each* cinnamon and nutmeg, ½ teaspoon *each* cloves, allspice, and soda; add to creamed mixture, mixing well. Stir in ½ cup mixed chopped candied fruits and peels and ½ cup slivered blanched almonds. Chill several hours or overnight.

Roll to ¼ inch on floured surface; cut in 3½x2-inch rectangles. Bake on greased cooky sheet at 350° about 12 minutes. Cool slightly before removing from pan. While warm spread with Lemon Glaze. Cool before storing—best if kept at least a few days in airtight container. Makes about 2 dozen.

Lemon Glaze: Combine 1 slightly beaten egg white, ½ teaspoon grated lemon peel, 1 tablespoon lemon juice, 1½ cups sifted confectioners' sugar, and dash salt.

Luscious holiday goodies

← It wouldn't be Christmas without Grandma's Fudge, Gingerbread Boys, Lebkuchen (with Kris Kringle cutouts), and Popcorn Balls.

Popcorn Balls

Prepare one recipe Popcorn Balls, page 38. To garland your Christmas tree, shape into tiny balls. Using a darning needle, string on baby ribbon.

Sugarplum Bread—Round Loaves

2 packages active dry yeast
½ cup *warm* water
1 cup milk, scalded
½ cup sugar
¼ cup shortening
1½ teaspoons salt
4¾ to 5¼ cups sifted all-purpose flour
1 teaspoon grated lemon peel
2 beaten eggs
1½ cups mixed diced candied fruits
    and peels
1 recipe Confectioners' Icing

Soften active dry yeast in *warm* water. Combine hot milk, sugar, shortening, and salt. Cool to lukewarm. Add 2 *cups* of the flour and the lemon peel; beat till smooth. Add eggs; beat well. Stir in softened yeast. Add fruits and peels. Stir in remaining flour (or enough to make a soft dough). Cover; let rest 10 minutes.

Knead on lightly floured surface till smooth and elastic (6 to 8 minutes). Place in lightly greased bowl, turning once to grease surface. Cover; let rise in warm place till double (about 2 hours). Punch down. Divide dough in half; round each into ball. Cover and let rest 10 minutes.

Place round loaves on greased cooky sheet; pat tops to flatten slightly. Cover and let rise till almost double (about 1½ hours). Bake in moderate oven (350°) about 25 to 30 minutes. (Cover tops with foil after 15 to 20 minutes to prevent overbrowning.) Cool on rack. While still slightly warm, glaze with Confectioners' Icing and decorate with bits of red and green candied cherries. Makes 2.

Tiny Sugarplum Loaves: Divide dough in half, then form each piece in 6 balls; shape in tiny loaves and place in 12 greased 4½x2½x1½-inch loaf pans. Let rise till almost double. Bake in moderate oven (350°) about 20 to 22 minutes, covering with foil after 15 minutes. (Or make 1 round and 6 little loaves.)

Sugar Cookies

Just like Grandma used to make—

1 cup butter or margarine
1 teaspoon vanilla
1½ cups sugar
3 eggs
3½ cups sifted all-purpose flour
2 teaspoons cream of tartar
1 teaspoon soda
½ teaspoon salt

Cream butter and vanilla. Add sugar gradually, creaming till light and fluffy. Add eggs, one at a time, beating after each. Sift dry ingredients together. Add gradually to creamed mixture. Chill *thoroughly* (3 to 4 hours).

Roll on well-floured surface to ⅛ to ¼ inch. Cut in desired shapes. (Want to hang cookies on tree? Then make a hole with a toothpick near top of each cooky before baking.) Bake on ungreased cooky sheets in moderate oven (375°) 6 to 8 minutes. Cool slightly on cooky sheet; remove to rack and finish cooling.

Decorate with colored sugar, decorettes, or halved candied cherries before baking or while still warm after baking. Or when cool, glaze or pipe with Confectioners' Icing. Makes about 8 dozen cookies.

Note: Instead of butter or margarine you may use shortening and increase salt to 1 teaspoon.

Treats for holiday nibbling!

Visions of sugarplums come true! Pass drop-in guests a holly-trimmed tray filled with Santatime treats. On the top deck are bright green and red Christmas Balls, and Swedish Spritz. The lower deck offers Almond Wreaths, Sugar Cookies (in many shapes—stars, Christmas trees, snowflakes), and Lattice Fruit Bars (the famous lattice-and-jam-topped Linzer cookies of Austria). Good to the last crumb!

Christmas Balls

1 cup butter or margarine
2 teaspoons vanilla

• • •

⅓ cup sugar
2 teaspoons water
2 cups sifted all-purpose flour
1 cup chopped pecans
Red and green sugar

Cream butter and vanilla; add sugar, creaming the mixture until light and fluffy. Blend in water. Stir in flour, mixing well. Add pecans. Shape in 1-inch balls. Roll in colored sugar.

Bake 1 inch apart on ungreased cooky sheet in slow oven (325°) 20 minutes or until firm to the touch. Cool before removing from pan. Makes 3 dozen.

Lattice Fruit Bars

1½ cups sifted all-purpose flour
¼ cup granulated sugar
½ teaspoon baking powder
½ teaspoon salt
½ teaspoon cinnamon
½ cup brown sugar
½ cup butter or margarine
1 slightly beaten egg
⅓ cup blanched almonds, ground

• • •

½ cup red-raspberry jam
1 slightly beaten egg yolk
1 teaspoon water

Sift together flour, sugar, baking powder, salt, and cinnamon; stir in brown sugar. Cut in butter till mixture is crumbly. Add egg and ground almonds; mix with fork. Reserve ½ cup mixture for lattice and into it mix 2 tablespoons additional flour; chill 1 hour.

Meanwhile press remaining mixture evenly into 9x9x2-inch pan. Spread with raspberry jam. Roll out reserved mixture on well-floured surface to ¼ inch. Cut in strips a little less than ¼-inch wide.

For lattice top, line up 11 strips across filling; then lay 11 strips diagonally across. Combine egg yolk and water; brush over lattice for glaze. Bake in moderate oven (375°) about 25 minutes or till done. Decorate with bits of red and green candied cherries. Cool. Cut in bars or squares.

Swedish Spritz (*Spritsar*)

Traditional in wreath or "S" shapes—

1½ cups butter or margarine
1 cup sugar
1 egg
1 teaspoon vanilla
½ teaspoon almond extract

• • •

4 cups sifted all-purpose flour
1 teaspoon baking powder

Thoroughly cream butter or margarine and sugar. Add egg, vanilla, and almond extract; beat well. Sift together flour and baking powder; add gradually to creamed mixture, mixing to a smooth dough.

Force dough through cooky press onto ungreased cooky sheet. Bake in hot oven (400°) 8 to 10 minutes. Cool thoroughly. Decorate. Makes about 6 dozen.

Almond Wreaths

Luscious and rich—

Cookies:

1 cup butter or margarine
½ cup granulated sugar
2½ cups sifted all-purpose flour

Filling:

½ cup finely chopped blanched
  almonds
1 tablespoon honey
⅓ cup brown sugar
1 egg, slightly beaten
Dash salt

Cookies: Cream butter; gradually add granulated sugar, creaming till light and fluffy. Stir in flour. Chill for several hours.

On lightly floured surface, roll to ⅛ inch. Cut with 2-inch round cutter. Cut centers from half the 2-inch rounds with 1⅜-inch round cutter.

Filling: Combine remaining ingredients. Place 2-inch cooky rounds on ungreased cooky sheet; place cooky rims atop. Spoon in about ¾ teaspoon filling. (If desired, add chopped candied fruit to filling.)

Bake in moderate oven (350°) for 15 minutes or till cookies are very lightly browned and filling is set. Remove to cooling rack. Makes about 3 dozen.